MINERALS

BY ROBERTA BAXTER

Published by The Child's World®
1980 Lookout Drive • Mankato, MN 56003-1705
800-599-READ • www.childsworld.com

Acknowledgments
The Child's World®: Mary Swensen, Publishing Director
Red Line Editorial: Editorial direction and production
The Design Lab: Design

Design Element: Shutterstock Images
Photographs ©: Shutterstock Images, cover (top), cover (bottom left), cover (bottom right), 1 (top), 1 (bottom left), 1 (bottom right), 17, 19, 20, 21; iStockphoto, 4, 6, 7, 9, 11, 23; Carlos Velayos/Shutterstock Images, 10; Pamela D. Maxwell/Shutterstock Images, 12; Marcel Clemens/Shutterstock Images, 13; Nastya Pirieva/Shutterstock Images, 14; Mark S. Johnson/Shutterstock Images, 15

ISBN 9781503808034
LCCN 2015958150

Printed in the United States of America
Mankato, MN
June, 2016
PA02305

ABOUT THE AUTHOR

Roberta Baxter has written more than 30 books for children and students of all ages. She writes most often about science and history. Baxter lives in Colorado.

CONTENTS

CHAPTER 1

What Are Minerals?

Picture a rock collection. One rock is gray with black specks. Another is white and shiny. A third rock is red with jagged edges. The rocks look different. They have varied colors and shapes. They are from different places, too. But they are all made of minerals.

Minerals are substances that occur naturally. They do not come from animals or plants.

Each type of mineral has a different combination of **elements**. Some minerals have only one element.

Rocks made of different minerals have different textures and colors.

Pure gold is an example of a mineral with one element. Most minerals are compounds. That means they include more than one element. The **atoms** of the different elements bond together. They form molecules.

You can find minerals almost everywhere. Our planet's **crust** is the thin top layer of Earth. It is made up of rocks and soil. Both rocks and soil are made up of minerals. Each rock has a mixture of minerals. Scientists can study the mixture to learn what kind of rock it is. Often, the minerals are not mixed together evenly. Instead, a rock has clumps of different minerals. Over time, rocks break down and turn into soil. The soil is also made of minerals.

A NEW MINERAL

Scientists are still finding new minerals. In April 2014, putnisite was discovered. This mineral is pink or purple. It contains several elements. These include sulfur, carbon, oxygen, and hydrogen. Putnisite was found in an isolated area in Australia.

To picture minerals inside rocks, think of a raisin cinnamon roll. The dough is the main mineral in the rock. The raisins are chunks of one kind of mineral. The cinnamon stripes are a layer of another mineral. Rocks can contain many types of minerals.

There are between 4,000 and 5,000 kinds of minerals on Earth. They are found in all types of rocks. One common mineral is quartz. Quartz is found in sandstone and in granite. Granite is an **igneous rock**. Sandstone is a **sedimentary rock**. Another common mineral is halite. This mineral is used in table salt. Halite is found around the world in sedimentary rocks. **Metamorphic rock** also contains minerals. Marble is one type of metamorphic rock. Some buildings and sculptures are made of marble. The minerals in marble are from the elements calcium, carbon, and oxygen.

Some minerals are **gems**. These minerals are prized for their beauty. People use these minerals in jewelry. Diamonds, emeralds, and rubies are all examples of gems.

Emeralds are one type of gem.

Minerals can form **crystals** bound together in a pattern. But not all crystals are minerals. Sugar is an organic compound that forms crystals. An organic compound is made from living things.

The most common mineral is called feldspar. It is made mostly of aluminum and silicon. It includes small amounts of other elements, such as potassium, calcium, and sodium. Feldspar rocks are different colors because of

This rock contains feldspar and granite. Feldspar is the most common mineral.

ELEMENTS IN MINERALS

Eight elements make up most minerals and rocks on Earth. This chart shows the most common elements in minerals.

Element	Percentage in Earth's Crust
Oxygen	47.2%
Silicon	28.2%
Aluminum	8.2%
Iron	5.1%
Calcium	3.7%
Sodium	2.9%
Potassium	2.6%
Magnesium	2.1%

this variety of elements. A feldspar rock that contains potassium will be white or pink. One that contains sodium may be red or yellow.

There are many kinds of minerals. They form in several different ways. Determining how minerals form helps scientists understand each mineral's traits.

CHAPTER 2

How Do Minerals Form?

Minerals are formed through processes that occur in Earth's crust and below Earth's surface. Some minerals form inside volcanoes. A substance called **magma** pushes up from under the surface. As it cools, it begins to form mineral crystals. The crystals are made up of chemical elements from the magma. Different volcanoes may contain different elements.

If the magma cools slowly, it forms large crystals. Topaz, a gem, is found in volcanic rock that cooled slowly. If the magma cools more quickly, the crystals are smaller. Obsidian, a black

Topaz forms from magma. Often, topaz is cut and polished to create jewelry.

GEODES

Geodes look like ordinary rocks on the outside. On the inside, they are full of sparkly crystals. Geodes often form from gas bubbles in hot magma. As the magma cools, the gas disappears. Water, carrying minerals, drips into the bubbles. The minerals crystallize inside the geode as the water leaks back out.

rock, forms from magma that cools quickly. People in ancient times used obsidian to make tools.

Minerals also form in water. Many different substances dissolve in water. As the water **evaporates**, these substances are left behind. They become solid minerals. In New Mexico, many rocks contain a mineral called gypsum. Mountains in this area contain gypsum as well. Over time, the rocks and mountains wear down. The gypsum dissolves and mixes with rain water. The water carries the

Gypsum is a soft mineral that can dissolve in water.

Gypsum crystals form in a cave.

dissolved gypsum down the mountains to a lake. As the water evaporates, the gypsum is left behind as white crystals. The wind picks up the crystals. It moves them to new places.

After minerals are formed, they often react with their environment. Sometimes, they form new minerals. Copper is a bright metal used in pennies. When copper is exposed to the air, it combines with oxygen. A new mineral, cuprite, forms a greenish crust.

Heat and pressure can transform one mineral into another mineral. Layers of rock push minerals underground. As the minerals are forced deeper, the pressure increases. Sometimes, other elements from nearby rock combine with the minerals. The pressure pushes them together. Ruby, a rare gem, is formed in this way.

Some rocks have only two or three kinds of minerals. Others have many more. Scientists can study the rocks to identify the minerals. Traits such as color and shape provide clues.

Pennies are made from copper and zinc.

CHAPTER 3

Types of Minerals

Minerals have different shapes, colors, and textures. Scientists identify minerals based on their traits. The elements in a mineral give its crystals a specific shape. Minerals such as pyrite and halite have cubic crystals. Quartz crystals have a **rhomboid** structure.

Minerals can also be identified by their color. Erythrite has a violet-red color from cobalt atoms. A green or blue mineral usually contains copper. Azurite is a mineral that contains copper atoms. It is a deep blue color. The vivid colors of gems are from atoms bonded in the structure of their crystals. Rubies and sapphires are both forms of the mineral corundum. But rubies contain an

Erythrite is a mineral with a purplish red color.

FOOL'S GOLD

Some minerals look alike. One mineral, pyrite, is also known as fool's gold. Flakes of pyrite sparkle in rocks. Many people who find this mineral think they have found gold. Sometimes pyrite and gold are found close to each other. But these two minerals have different traits. Pyrite is harder than gold.

element called chromium. This element gives the rubies their red color. Sapphires get their blue color from iron and titanium.

There are several groups of minerals. Scientists categorize minerals based on the elements they contain. Minerals that have only one element are known as native elements. These kinds of minerals are rare. Other minerals have two or more elements. One category is known as silicates. This type of mineral always contains silicon and oxygen. Silicates may also contain other elements. Quartz is one example of a silicate. Another silicate is talc. This mineral is used in paper and roofing products.

Talc is a soft mineral used in many products.

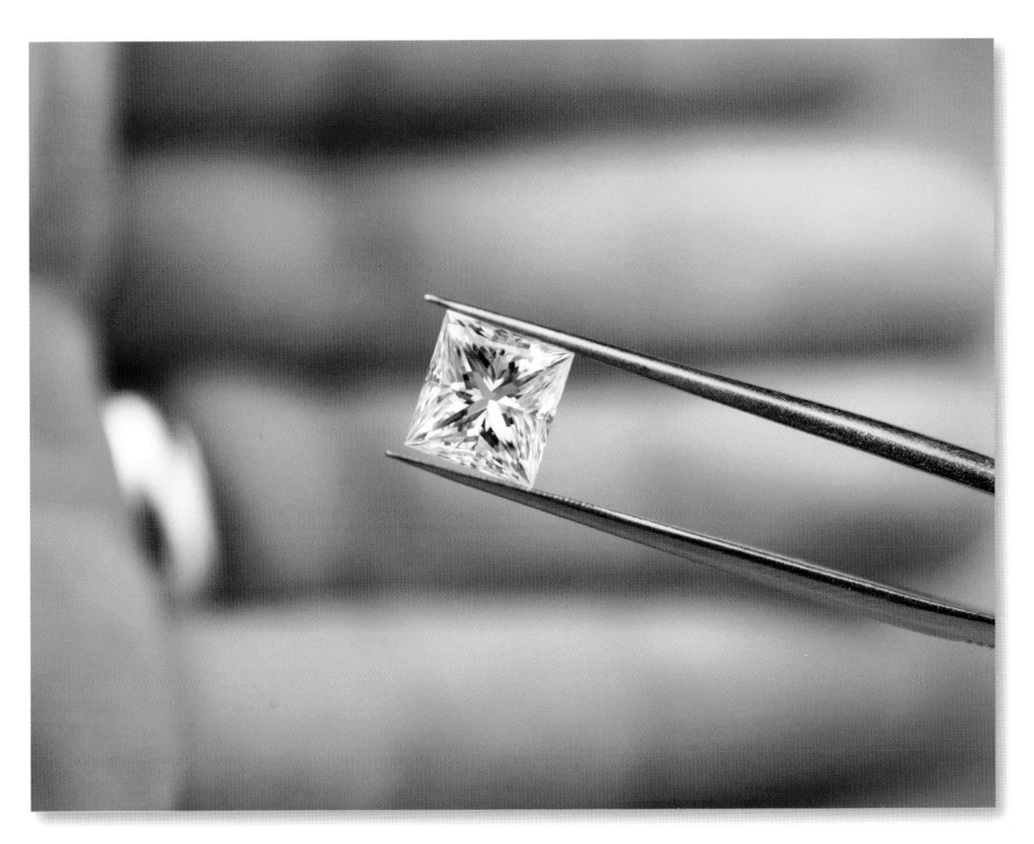

Diamond is the hardest mineral. Diamonds are prized for their beauty.

In 1812, a scientist found a new way to identify minerals. Friedrich Mohs created a scale of mineral hardness. The scale measures how difficult it is to scratch each mineral. Talc is the softest mineral. It is so soft that it can be scratched with a person's fingernail. Diamond is the hardest mineral. It can only be scratched by another diamond. A mineral can be scratched by any mineral higher on the scale.

MOHS SCALE OF MINERAL HARDNESS

Each mineral has a number on the Mohs scale. The minerals in this chart are just some of the minerals found on Earth.

Number	Mineral	What Can Scratch It
1	Talc	Fingernail
2	Gypsum	Fingernail
3	Calcite	Bronze Coin
4	Fluorite	Iron Nail
5	Apatite	Glass
6	Orthoclase	Knife
7	Quartz	Steel File
8	Topaz	Emery Sandpaper
9	Corundum	Knife Sharpener
10	Diamond	Diamond

Minerals have many colors and shapes. Some are hard and some are soft. These traits affect how the minerals look and feel. A mineral's traits also determine how it can be used. Different types of minerals have different uses. We use many minerals every day.

CHAPTER 4

Everyday Uses for Minerals

Every day, people use minerals. You probably use many minerals each morning. Perhaps you start the day by washing up. You brush your teeth. Then you wash your hair. Toothpaste is made from limestone, mica, and talc. All of these are minerals. Shampoos are made from minerals, too. So are other soaps.

The gasoline people use for cars is a mineral product.

COLLECTING MINERALS

Many people collect minerals as a hobby. They use a geologist's hammer and brushes to clean rocks. A strainer helps them separate samples. Safety gear, including helmets and eye protection, is also important. The best way to start collecting is to go with an experienced guide. The guide can explain where to look for minerals.

You use other minerals when you eat breakfast. Plates and bowls are made from clay mudstone or feldspar. Do you sprinkle salt on your food? Table salt is made from the mineral halite.

After breakfast, you might get a ride to school. Cars and buses use gasoline and oil. Both are mineral products. A car battery contains several minerals, including lead and sulfur. The car's window is made of glass. This glass comes from the minerals feldspar and silica. Even the paint on the car comes from minerals. Asphalt roads and sidewalks are made from rock product. Cement is made from the mineral limestone.

Think about what you do at school. The materials you use probably contain minerals. Your plastic pencil case is made of minerals. In fact, it contains the same minerals found in cars. Do you use a computer? Its insides have

Pencil lead is made from the mineral graphite.

metal pieces made from silver, gold, and copper. Your school uses electricity that travels through copper wires.

Even the pages in your textbook contain minerals, in addition to paper pulp from trees. The pages are made with kaolin clay, limestone, and soda ash. Do you use chalk? Chalk is made with limestone, too. Your pencil lead contains a mineral called graphite.

People use minerals at work, school, and home. Farmers rely on fertilizers to grow vegetables. These fertilizers contain the minerals phosphate and potash. Repair workers use tools such as blades and saws. Often, these tools include diamond. The hardness of the mineral helps the tools cut other materials.

Companies retrieve minerals by mining them. Workers mine copper in the United States. They also

In Rio Tinto, Spain, workers mine copper from the earth.

mine zinc, iron, and other minerals. Minerals are often imported. The United States gets silver from Mexico and Peru. Heavy mining can harm the environment. It can pollute the water and air. But it also has benefits. Mining is how we obtain products we use in our daily lives.

Some minerals are common. Others are rare. Scientists are still making discoveries about minerals. They are finding new uses for minerals, too. Many are used in new technology. Minerals make our lives easier. Our lives would not be the same without them.

The United States both mines silver and imports silver from other countries.

GLOSSARY

atoms *(AT-umz)* Atoms are the smallest particles of an element that have all the properties of the element. The copper atoms bonded to the oxygen atoms.

crust *(KRUST)* The crust is Earth's outermost layer. Earth's crust is made of soil and rock.

crystallize *(KRIS-tuh-lyze)* To crystallize is to form crystals. Minerals may crystallize in water.

crystals *(KRIS-tulz)* Solids that form in a regular pattern are called crystals. Diamonds are crystals of carbon that formed under high heat and pressure.

elements *(EL-uh-muntz)* Elements are substances that cannot be broken into a simpler substance. Minerals may contain several elements.

evaporates *(ih-VAP-uh-reyts)* When a liquid evaporates, it changes into a vapor or gas. When water evaporates, it may leave behind solid minerals.

gems *(JEMZ)* Crystallized minerals that are valued for their beauty are called gems. Diamonds, emeralds, and rubies are gems.

igneous rock *(IG-nee-us ROK)* Igneous rock is formed from melted magma or lava. The magma hardens into igneous rock.

magma *(MAG-muh)* Magma is hot melted rock from inside Earth. When magma cools, the minerals inside it harden into crystals.

metamorphic rock *(met-uh-MOR-fik ROK)* Metamorphic rock is transformed igneous or sedimentary rock. Heat or pressure can cause metamorphic rock to form.

rhomboid *(ROM-boyd)* In a rhomboid shape, there are four sides but only the opposite sides are equal to each other. Sulfur crystals often form in a rhomboid shape.

sedimentary rock *(sed-i-MEN-tuh-ree ROK)* Sedimentary rock forms from sediment carried by water or air. Often, sedimentary rock forms near seas or lakes.

TO LEARN MORE

IN THE LIBRARY

Dee, Willa. ***Minerals***. New York: PowerKids, 2014.

Pocket Genius: Rocks and Minerals. New York: DK Publishing, 2012.

Squire, Ann O. ***Minerals***. New York: Scholastic, 2012.

Tomecek, Steve. ***Everything Rocks and Minerals***. Washington, DC: National Geographic, 2011.

ON THE WEB

Visit our Web site for links about minerals: **childsworld.com/links**

Note to Parents, Teachers, and Librarians: We routinely verify our Web links to make sure they are safe and active sites. So encourage your readers to check them out!

INDEX